635   Esbaum, Jill.
ESB   Seed, sprout,
             pumpkin, pie

         BAR: 32489120005811

PERMA-BOUND

DATE DUE			

Seed, Sprout, Pumpkin, Pie

BY JILL ESBAUM

Pumpkins

For Christopher Lauren

Published by the National Geographic Society
1145 17th Street N.W.
Washington, D.C. 20036-4688

Library of Congress Cataloging-in-Publication Data

Esbaum, Jill.
 Seed, sprout, pumpkin, pie / by Jill Esbaum. -- 1st ed.
    p. cm.
 ISBN 978-1-4263-0582-5 (pbk. : alk. paper)
 1. Pumpkin--Juvenile literature. I. Title.
 QK495.C96E83 2009
 635'.62--dc22

                                    2009012735

Printed in USA

09/WOR/1

Have you picked
your pumpkin?

A pumpkin seed
is tucked into
sun-warmed earth.
Spring rains soften
its tough coat.

A root reaches
for nutrients.
A sprout reaches
for light.

Soon jagged leaves
rise from twisty
vines wandering in
all directions.

They can be green, red, tan, yellow, white, or even blue.

The pumpkins we know best are bright orange.

There are **tall** pumpkins. SHORT pumpkins.

Smooth or bumpy pumpkins.

wee ones, only inches wide,
or GIANTS you can
sit inside.

Thump-thump-thump.

A pumpkin sounds hollow, but inside is stringy wet pulp and oodles of slippery white seeds.

Seeds might be saved to grow next year's pumpkins or dried for a crunchy snack.

Pumpkin pulp smells
sharp and tangy, but
can be made into
delicious breads,
desserts, and soups.

Sugar
pumpkins
go into the
spicy pies we
bring to our
Thanksgiving
tables.

The End.

Unless... was there something
else pumpkins might be used for?

Oh, yes.
Jack-'o-lanterns!

Will you give yours a funny face or a creepy one to send shivers up your back?

Will it be the head of a straw-filled scarecrow?

Will your Jack-'o-lantern decorate your kitchen table among striped gourds and sunset-colored leaves?

Or will it set your porch aglow on a spooky Halloween night, lighting the way for a curious cat?

Unused pumpkins
are fed to farm
animals or left in the
field to nourish the
precious soil...

...awaiting spring under
a wintry blanket.

Published by the National Geographic Society

John M. Fahey, Jr., *President and Chief Executive Officer*
Gilbert M. Grosvenor, *Chairman of the Board*
Tim T. Kelly, *President, Global Media Group*
John Q. Griffin, *Executive Vice President; President, Publishing*
Nina D. Hoffman, *Executive Vice President; President, Book Publishing Group*
Melina Gerosa Bellows, *Executive Vice President, Children's Publishing*

Prepared by the Book Division

Nancy Laties Feresten, *Vice President, Editor in Chief, Children's Books;* Bea Jackson, *Director of Design and Illustrations, Children's Books;* Amy Shields, *Executive Editor, Series, Children's Books;* Jennifer Emmett, *Executive Editor, Reference and Solo, Children's Books;* Carl Mehler, *Director of Maps;* R. Gary Colbert, *Production Director;* Jennifer A. Thornton, *Managing Editor*

Staff for This Book

Becky Baines, *Project Editor;* James Hiscott, Jr., *Art Director/ Designer;* Lori Epstein Renda, *Illustrations Editor;* Grace Hill, *Asst. Managing Editor;* Lewis R. Bassford, *Production Manager;* Susan Borke, *Legal and Business Affairs*

Manufacturing and Quality Management

Christopher A. Liedel, *Chief Financial Officer;* Phillip L. Schlosser, *Vice President;* Chris Brown, *Technical Director;* Rachel Faulise, *Manager*

Original design by Molly Leach

1, SW Productions/ Photodisc/ Getty Images; 2 left, Roger Phillips/ Dorling Kindersley; 2 top right, Michael Newman/ Photo Edit; 2 bottom right, Terry Vacha/ Alamy Ltd; 2 right, Natasha Litova/ iStockphoto.com; 3, Jose B. Ruiz / naturepl.com; 4 top, Corey Hochachka/ Robertstock.com; 4 bottom, Will Heap/ Dorling Kindersley; 5, Marilyn Volan/ Shutterstock; 6, Ed Bailey/ Associated Press; 7 top, Peter Arnold, Inc./ Alamy Ltd; 7 bottom, John Robertson/ Alamy Ltd; 8 top, John Henley/ Corbis; 8 bottom, Masterfile; 9, Sol Neelman/ Corbis; 10 top, Doug Berry/Corbis; 10 bottom left, Norm Dettlaff/ Las Cruces Sun-News/ Associated Press; 10 bottom right, Simon Krzic/ Shutterstock; 11 top, Richard Jung/FoodPix/ Jupiter Images; 11 bottom, Ryan McVay/ Photodisc/ Getty Images; 12, Richard Nowitz/ NationalGeographicStock.com; 13 top, O'Brien Productions/Corbis; 13 bottom, 14 top, Andre Baranowski/ Images.com/ ipnstock.com; Jason Lindsey/ Alamy Ltd; 14 center, Phil Schermeister/ NationalGeographicStock.com; 14 bottom, Eric Isselée/ iStockphoto.com; 15 top, Mark Gutma/ The Batavia Daily News/ Associated Press; 15 bottom, Jayne Hinds Bidaut/Graphistock/ Jupiter Images; 16, William A. Bake/ Corbis; Cover, Raimund Linke/ Roam Images/ Jupiter Images

For more information, please call 1-800-NGS LINE (647-5463) or write to the following address:
National Geographic Society
1145 17th Street N.W.
Washington, D.C. 20036-4688 U.S.A.

Visit us online at www.nationalgeographic.com/books
For librarians and teachers: www.ngchildrensbooks.org
More for kids from National Geographic: kids.nationalgeographic.com

For information about special discounts for bulk purchases, please contact National Geographic Books Special Sales: ngspecsales@ngs.org

For rights or permissions inquiries, please contact National Geographic Books Subsidiary Rights: ngbookrights@ngs.org

Pumpkins

Brand new from National Geographic's
Picture the Seasons

And don't forget your other Picture the Season favorites

NATIONAL
GEOGRAPHIC